Davy Crockett

A True American Hero

By Kaitlyn Nichols

HAMERAY
PUBLISHING GROUP

Published in the United States of America
by the Hameray Publishing Group, Inc.

Text © 2009, 2013 Kaitlyn Nichols
Maps © 2009 Hameray Publishing Group, Inc.
First Published 2009
Revised Edition 2013

Publisher: Raymond Yuen
Series Editors: Adria F. Klein and Alan Trussell-Cullen
Project Editor: Kaitlyn Nichols
Designers: Lois Stanfield and Linda Lockowitz
Map Designer: Barry Age

Photo Credits: Corbis: front cover and pages 1, 8, 12, 14, 19, 22, 30, 33
Getty: back cover and pages 4, 16, 28–29
SuperStock: page 26

ISBN 978-1-60559-057-8

Printed in China

2 3 4 5 6 CP 17 16 15 14 13

Contents

4

Chapter 1

A True American Hero

Everyone dreams of having adventures. But one man had more real adventures in his lifetime than most people ever dream about. Davy Crockett was that man. He had adventures as a **frontiersman**. He had adventures as a lawmaker. He had adventures as a soldier.

Davy grew up in the backwoods of Tennessee. He barely went to school. But he became famous for his adventures. Though he liked to be called "David," people began to call him "Davy" when they told stories of his adventures.

◄ Davy Crockett as a young man.

People still love hearing about Davy Crockett's adventures. There have been books, movies, and songs about him. Over the years, tall tales have been added to the story of Davy Crockett's life. But the real story of his life proves that he had enough adventures of his own to make him one of the first true American heroes.

Tall Tales

Tall tales are stories that are made up and shared through storytelling. Tall tales include unbelievable made-up parts to make the story more entertaining and interesting.

Chapter 2

Adventures As a Cowboy

Davy Crockett was born on August 17, 1786, in Greene County, Tennessee. His parents were poor **settlers** who moved around a lot, looking for ways to support their large family.

The family finally settled in Morristown, Tennessee. Davy's father opened a tavern where travelers often stopped to eat and stay the night.

▲ Davy Crockett's birthplace in Greene County, Tennessee.

Davy loved listening to the travelers' stories. He liked to hear about their adventures on the wild **frontier**. He dreamed about going there and having adventures, too.

Davy was young, but he needed to earn money to help his family. At twelve years old, Davy got his first job. He was hired as a

cowboy to help drive herds of cattle. It was very hard work for a young boy. But Davy liked being out on the trail and visiting new places. After almost a year, Davy became homesick and ran away. He went back to Greene County.

His father was not happy to see him. Davy's father told him that if he wasn't going to work to help the family, he had to start going to school.

Davy thought about returning to his job as a cowboy, but decided he needed to go to school and learn how to read and write. The next day, twelve-year-old Davy set off for school for the very first time.

At school, Davy was the new kid. He was also way behind the other kids his age. On his very first day, Davy got into a fight with a bully. Davy was afraid he would get in trouble with his teacher for fighting. Instead of going back to school, he got another job as a cowboy and set back out on the trail.

For the next few years, Davy's jobs took him to new and exciting places. When he finally returned home, his family didn't recognize him. But when his sister finally realized the fifteen-year-old was her brother, the family was overjoyed. Davy decided to stay in Tennessee and continued to work to help his family.

Davy knew that school was important, so he worked for a teacher in exchange for lessons. Davy was sixteen years old when he learned the alphabet and how to read and write. He also learned basic math, history, and geography. Altogether, Davy only attended about one hundred days of school in his whole life.

Chapter 3

Adventures As a Hunter

When Davy Crockett was eighteen, he bought his own horse and his first rifle for hunting. A year later, he met a pretty girl named Polly Finley. Davy Crockett and Polly Finley were married in 1806. They had two sons and a daughter. Crockett was always looking for new adventures. He moved his family to a log cabin on the Tennessee frontier.

Crockett supported his family by farming and by hunting deer, bears, and other animals. Crockett traded the animal skins for money and supplies. Paintings of Crockett show him in his hunting clothes, wearing a coonskin cap and holding a rifle.

He called his favorite rifle "Betsy." With Betsy, he was an excellent hunter and won many shooting contests. He claimed that in one season he shot 105 bears! Davy was a great hunter, but he was also a great storyteller.

▲ A painting of Davy Crockett in his hunting clothes with his dogs.

Chapter 4

Adventures As a Soldier

In the early 1800s, settlers in the Southeast were beginning to move into **Creek Indian** country. Sometimes, fights broke out between the settlers and the Indians because the settlers were moving onto Indian land. In 1813, Creek Indians attacked Fort Mims in Tennessee. This was the start of the Creek War.

Crockett **volunteered** to fight against the Indians. He believed that going to war was a duty he owed his country. Crockett was a **scout** under General Andrew Jackson. He was sent on missions to learn where the Creek Indians were hiding.

▲ General Andrew Jackson.

Andrew Jackson

Andrew Jackson was a general during the Creek War and was later elected as president of the United States. Jackson was nicknamed "Old Hickory" after the tough type of tree near his native North Carolina. He became a national hero as a major general during the War of 1812. He was America's seventh president, serving from 1829–1837.

On his scouting missions, Crockett often visited with the friendly Cherokee Indians. The Cherokees helped Crockett and the other soldiers. They let the soldiers camp with them and took Crockett hunting.

Crockett's time as a soldier was hard. The soldiers didn't have a lot of supplies or food. Davy hunted for animals to feed the soldiers. Without Davy's help, the soldiers would have starved.

▲ A woodcarving of the Creek Indians from around 1800.

On January 21, 1814, Crockett helped the Americans win a battle against the Creek Indians. Crockett was happy that they won, but he learned that he did not like fighting. He said he had "done Indian fighting enough for one time," and he headed home. Another adventure had come to an end for Davy Crockett.

> " . . . the enemy fought with savage fury, and met death with all its horrors without shrinking or complaining. Not one asked to be spared, but fought as long as they could stand."
>
> —Davy Crockett

Chapter 5

The Man of the People Becomes a Politician

After Davy Crockett returned home, Polly died from an unknown illness. He was very sad, but men at this time often remarried quickly to have someone to help look after their farms and families. In 1816, he married a widow named Elizabeth Patton. Together, they had three more children.

In 1817, Crockett moved his family to a new settlement in Shoal Creek, Tennessee. As the town grew, laws and lawmakers were needed. So Crockett began another adventure. He was elected to be a **justice of the peace**. He helped settle arguments. People respected Crockett. They thought his rulings were fair.

In 1821, Crockett ran for the Tennessee State **Legislature**. He wanted to become a lawmaker for the state. His **opponent**'s speeches were full of big words. But Crockett spoke plainly. He told the audience jokes and stories. He once memorized his opponent's speech and recited it for him! The audience thought this was funny. His opponent did not!

▲ Davy Crockett's funny speeches helped him win votes.

The settlers trusted Crockett. He understood their problems. He was "a man of the people." He was just like everyone else. They voted for him and he won the election. He was a Tennessee lawmaker for four years. He helped pass laws that would help poor settlers and farmers.

> *"I gave my decisions on the principles of common justice and honesty between man and man, and relied on natural born sense, and not on law; for I had never read a page in a law book in all my life."* —Davy Crockett

But while Crockett was helping his neighbors, he was having more troubles. He spent all of his money to build a mill that would grind flour and corn using the power of the river. Then the mill was destroyed in a flood. The family lost everything. It was time to move again.

Chapter 6

Congressman Crockett

Davy Crockett and his family settled on the Obion River in Tennessee. In 1827, Crockett decided to run for U.S. **Congress**. Once, a flock of birds chirped during a speech given by his opponent. He told the crowd that the birds were chanting "Crockett! Crockett!" His humor helped him win the election!

In Washington, D.C., Crockett worried that other **congressmen** would laugh at him. He was from the backwoods and had barely gone to school. Most congressmen were from cities and were well-educated. He wore hunting clothes. Congressmen wore fancy suits.

▲ Davy Crockett was elected as a congressman from Tennessee.

Some people did laugh, but Crockett ignored them. While Congress wasn't **impressed** with Congressman Crockett, the public couldn't get enough of him. A book about his life was published that contained tall tales, stories that couldn't possibly be true. Crockett decided to write his own book that would tell people the truth. He wrote about his life in Tennessee and his hunting adventures.

Davy Crockett called his book about his adventurous life: A Narrative of the Life of David Crockett of the State of Tennessee.

The book was printed in 1834 and was a big success. People even talked about him becoming the next president!

In Congress, Crockett fought for the poor people of Tennessee. But he had trouble working with other congressmen. Crockett didn't get along with one person in particular: his former general, who was now President Andrew Jackson.

Though Crockett had fought against the Indians in the Creek War, once he became a congressman, he supported the Indians' rights. He was against President Jackson's Indian Removal Act. The act forced Indians to leave their land and settle out west.

Crockett became known as "the **rebel** congressman." The voters wanted a congressman who would work with the president. After serving three terms, Crockett lost his next election. No one talked about President Crockett anymore.

> *"I am at liberty to vote as my conscience and judgment dictate to be right."* —Davy Crockett

Chapter 7

Defending the Alamo

Davy Crockett's political career was over. He needed a new start in a new place. As he had done as a teenager, he went in search of adventure on the frontier. He heard there was great hunting and good land in Texas. So Crockett headed west.

> "Texas is the richest country in the world: good land, plenty of timber, the best springs, and good mill streams. Good range, clear water, and every appearance of health—game aplenty." —Davy Crockett

Crockett loved Texas and decided it was the perfect place for his family. At the time, Texas was ruled by Mexico. American settlers wanted **independence** from Mexican rule. In 1836, Crockett volunteered to help Texas fight for its independence.

Crockett went to San Antonio with Colonel William B. Travis. Crockett's help was needed to fight against General Santa Ana, leader of the Mexican army. On February 23, 1836, 4,000 Mexican soldiers took over the city. There were only 180 Texan soldiers under Colonel Travis. The soldiers and their families retreated into a former **mission**, known as the Alamo.

The soldiers were outnumbered. They were tired and were running out of food. But Crockett and the other soldiers would not be **defeated**. They wanted freedom and independence. They fought hard to protect the Alamo for almost two weeks.

◄ The Alamo today, in San Antonio, Texas.

Before dawn on March 6, 1836, the Mexican army attacked the Alamo. By sunrise, every last man in the Alamo was dead. Davy Crockett was one of the brave soldiers

who lost his life fighting for the independence
of Texas.

This famous painting shows Davy Crockett
▼ fighting heroically at the Alamo.

Painted by A.L. De Rose.   Engraved by A.B. Durand.

I leave this rule, for others when I am dead
Be always, Sure, you are right, then go, a head

David Crockett

Chapter 8

"Remember the Alamo!"

Today, Davy Crockett's adventures are still famous. Songs, stories, and movies have been made about his life. In 1954, Disney made a movie called *Davy Crockett, King of the Wild Frontier*. Disney also made a television series about Davy Crockett and had a song written to tell of his life. The well-known song claims that Davy killed a bear when he was only three! Tall tales were mixed with the truth. The story of Davy Crockett soon turned into folklore.

◀ Davy Crockett signed this portrait with his most famous saying, "Be always sure you are right, then go ahead."

But the courage Davy Crockett and the Texans showed at the Alamo is not a made-up story. On April 21, 1836, General Santa Ana's army was defeated. Texas was on its way to independence! "Remember the Alamo!" has become a well-known saying. It is a reminder to never forget Davy Crockett and all those who fought for freedom in the early days of the United States.

This monument in San Antonio honors the volunteer ▶ soldiers from Texas who died defending the Alamo.

JAMES BUTLER BONHAM · JAMES BOWIE · JESSE B.BOWMAN · DA
IAM BLAZEBY · JAMES BUTLER BONHAM · ROBERT CROSSMAN · DAVID P. CUM
LEMUEL CRAWFORD · DAVID CROCKETT · SAMUEL B. EVANS · JAME
S ESPALIER · GREGORIO ESPARZA · ROBERT EVANS · JAMES C. GWIN
DIGH · ALFRED CALVIN GRIMES · JOSE MARIA GUERRERO · JAMES C. GWIN
EN.B JAMESON · GORDON C. JENNINGS · LEWIS JOHNSON · JOHN JONES · J

Timeline

1786   Davy Crockett is born in Greene County, Tennessee, August 17

1798   Leaves home for the first time to work as cowboy

1799   Starts school at age 12

1802   Learns to read and write at age 16

1806   Marries Polly Finley

1813   Enlists as a volunteer to fight in Creek War

1814   Helps win a battle against Creek Indians, January 21

1815   Ends his service as a volunteer soldier; Polly Crockett Dies

1816   Marries Elizabeth Patton

1817	Moves to Shoal Creek, Tennessee; becomes a justice of the peace
1821	Is elected to Tennessee State Legislature
1827	Is elected to U.S. Congress
1834	Publishes *A Narrative of the Life of David Crockett of the State of Tennessee*
1835	Loses his run for Congress; goes to Texas
1836	Dies at the Alamo on March 6; General Santa Ana is defeated in April
1845	Texas becomes a U.S. state
1954	Disney makes movie called *Davy Crockett, King of the Wild Frontier*

Glossary

Congress the chief lawmakers of a nation; in the U.S., Congress is made up of the Senate and the House of Representatives

congressmen members of Congress, lawmakers

cowboy someone who tends cattle or horses

Creek Indians an Indian tribe from the southeastern United States

defeated to win victory over or beat

frontier the far edge of a country, where people are just beginning to settle

frontiersman someone who works or lives on the far edge of a country

impressed	to gain the admiration or interest of
independence	freedom
justice of the peace	an elected official who acts as a judge
legislature	an elected body of people who make or change laws
mission	church
opponent	a person who fights or plays against another person
rebel	a person that goes against authority
scout	a person who is given the job of being a lookout or is sent ahead to spy on the enemy
settlers	people that live in a new place
volunteered	offered to work or help without pay

Learn More

Books

Davy Crockett: A Life on the Frontier by Stephen
  Krensky (Aladdin, 2004)
In Their Own Words: Davy Crockett by George
  Sullivan (Scholastic, 2002)
A Narrative of the Life of David Crockett by David
  Crockett (University of Nebraska Press, 1987
What's So Great About . . . ? Davy Crockett by
  Russell Roberts (Mitchell Lane Publishers, 2006)

Websites

www.aboutfamouspeople.com/article1024.html
www.thealamo.org

Movies

The Alamo starring John Wayne (1960)
The Alamo starring Billy Bob Thornton and Dennis
  Quaid (2004)
Davy Crockett starring Fess Parker (1950s)

Visit

The Alamo, San Antonio, Texas

Index